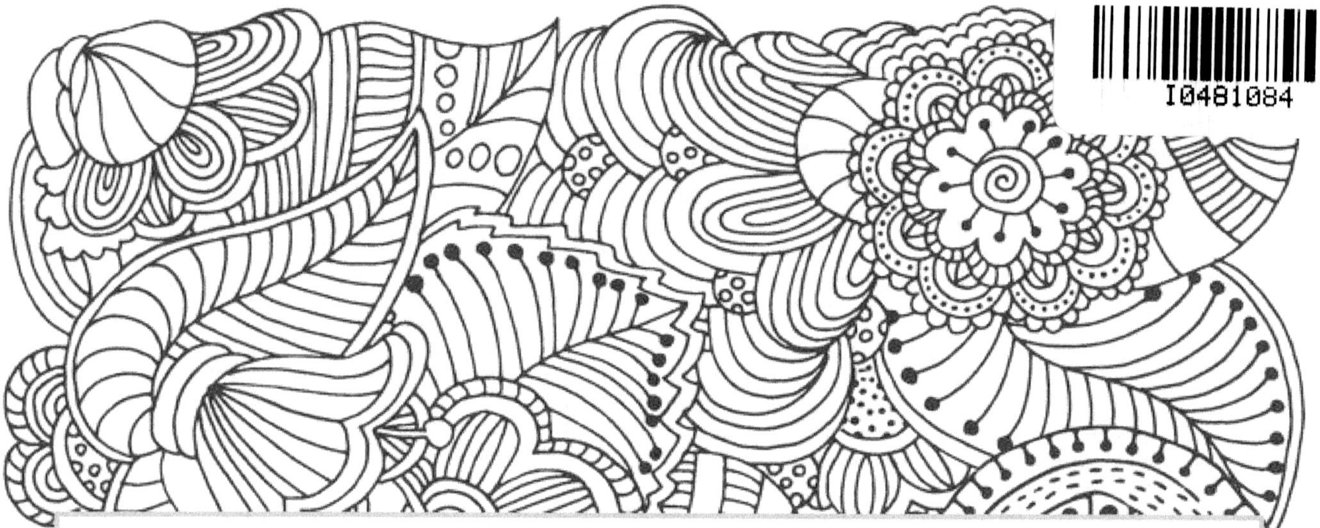

This book belongs to....

....

....

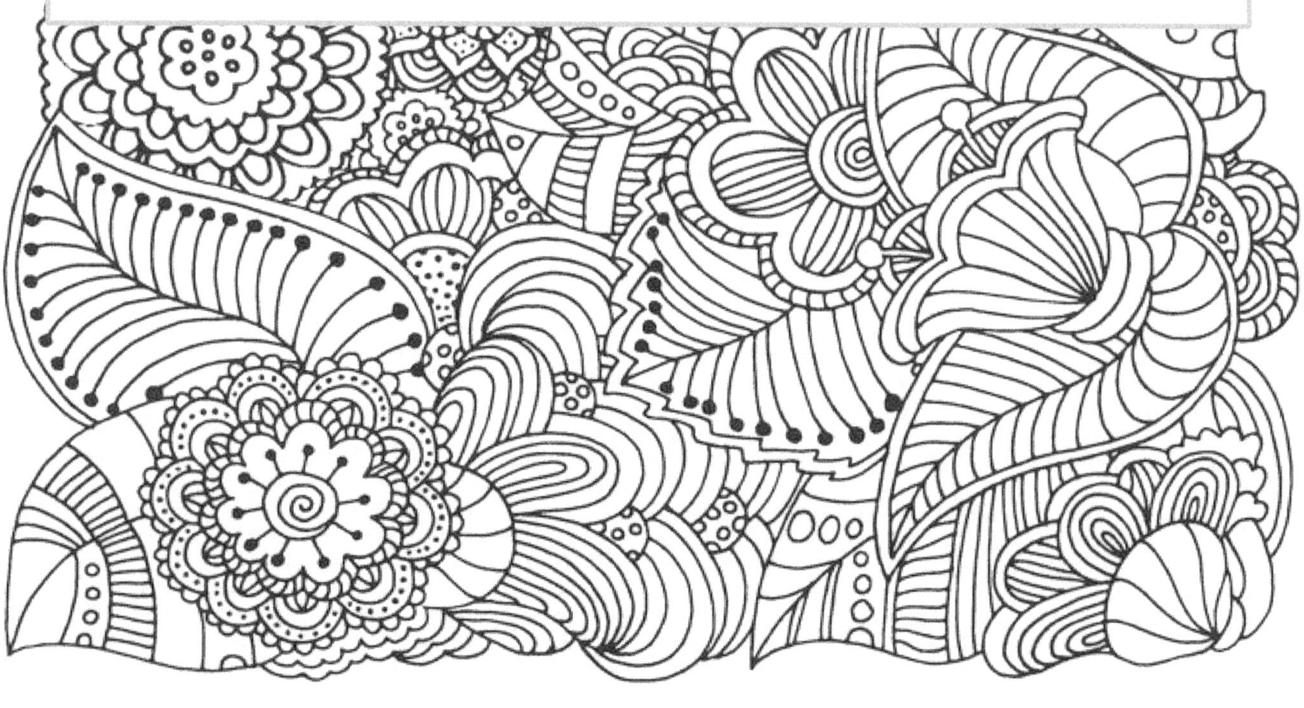

Small preview of what's inside

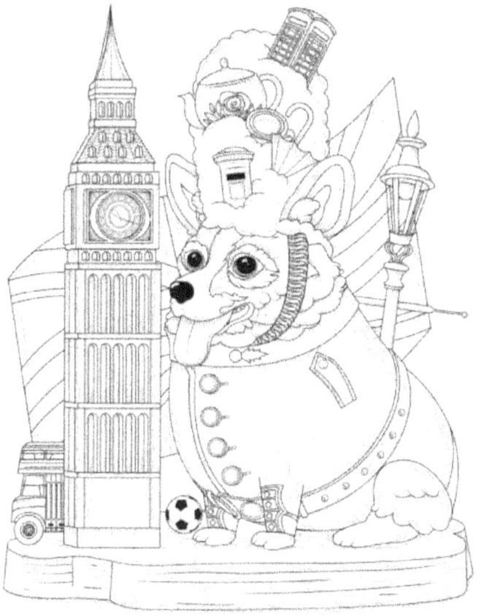

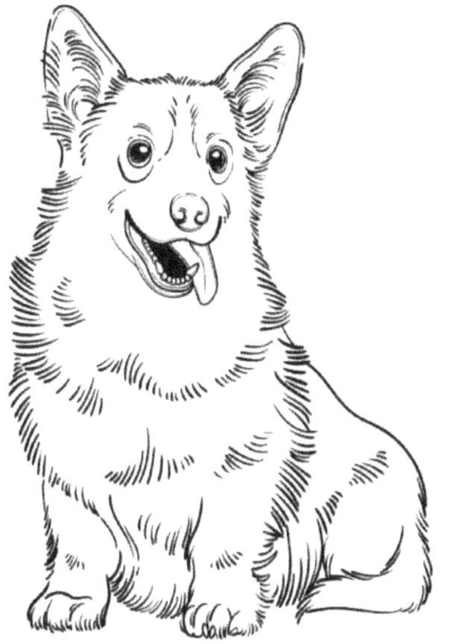

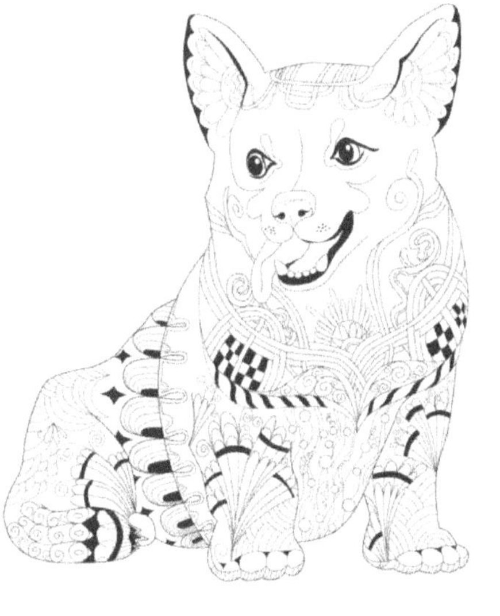

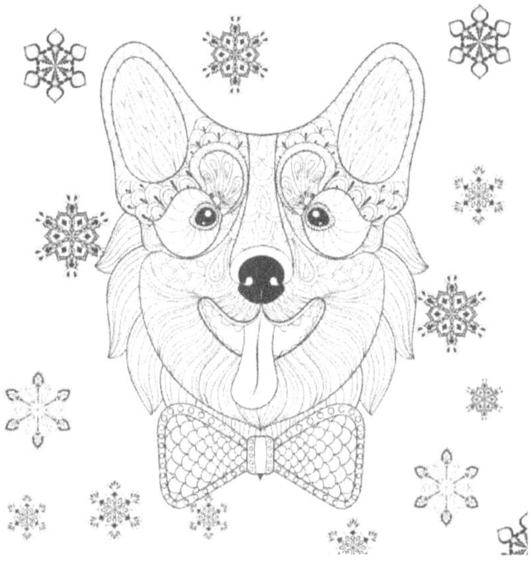

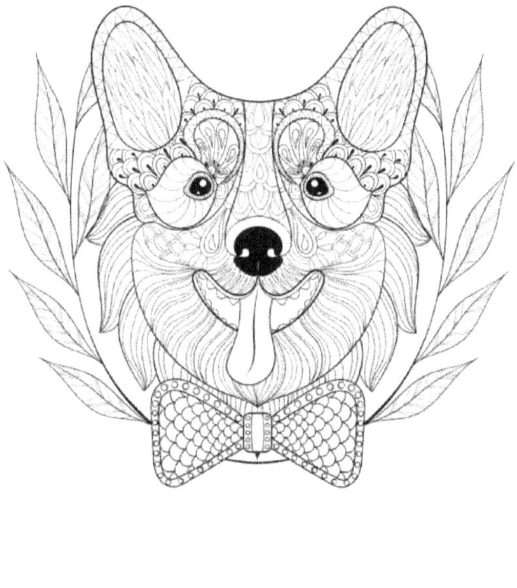

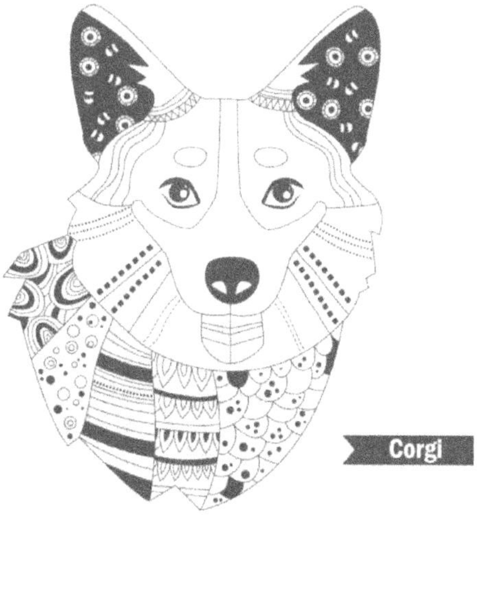

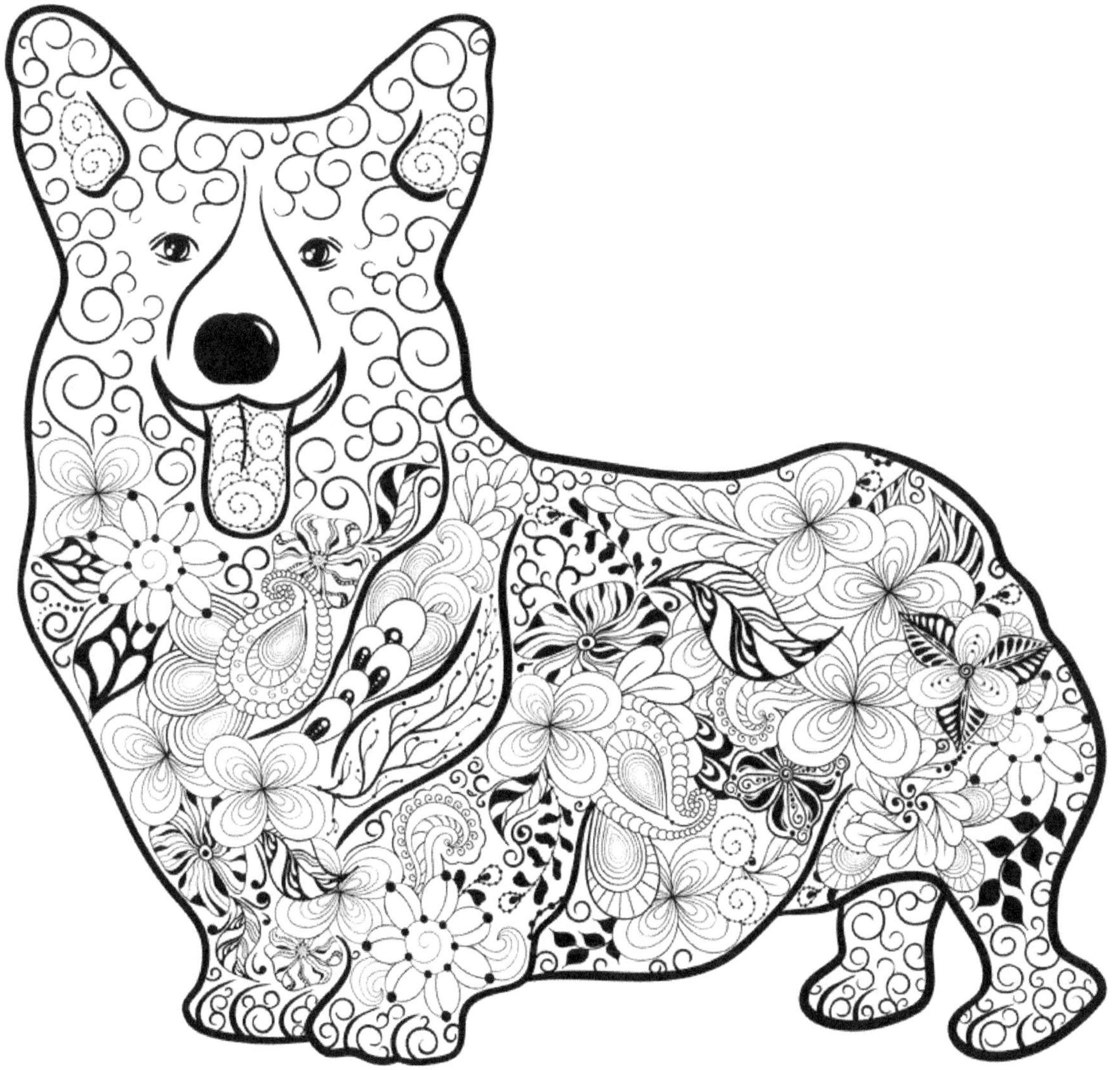

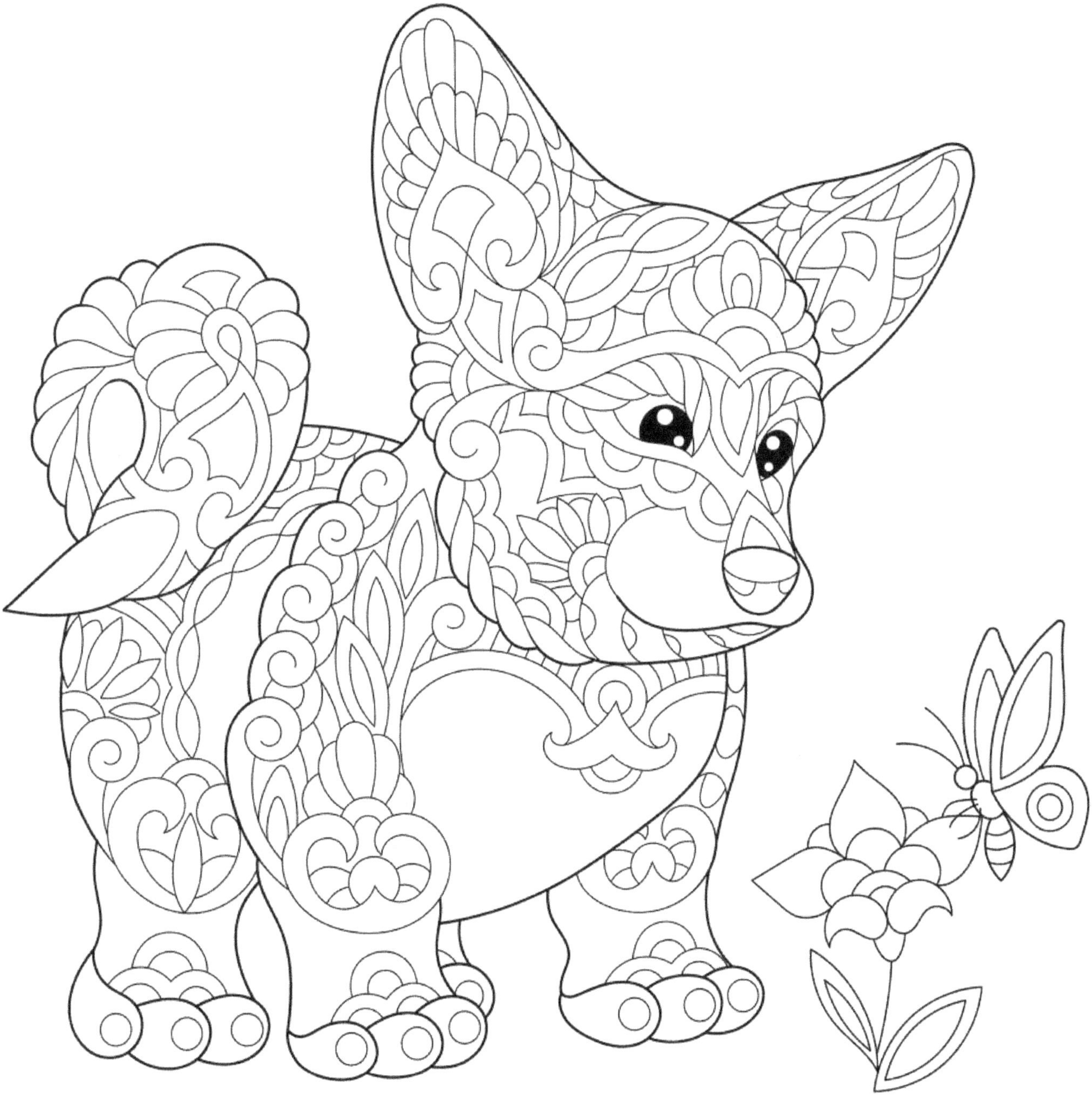

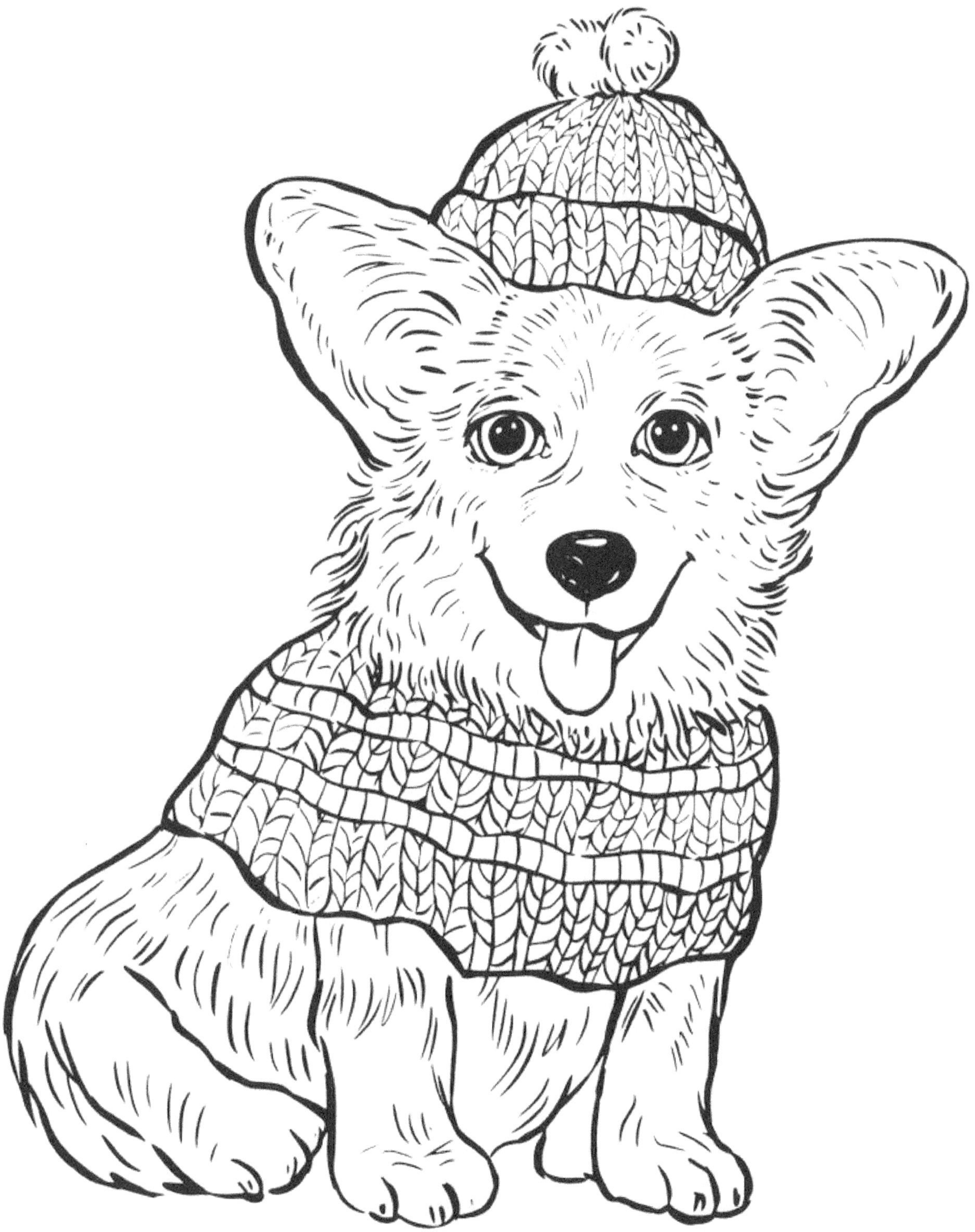

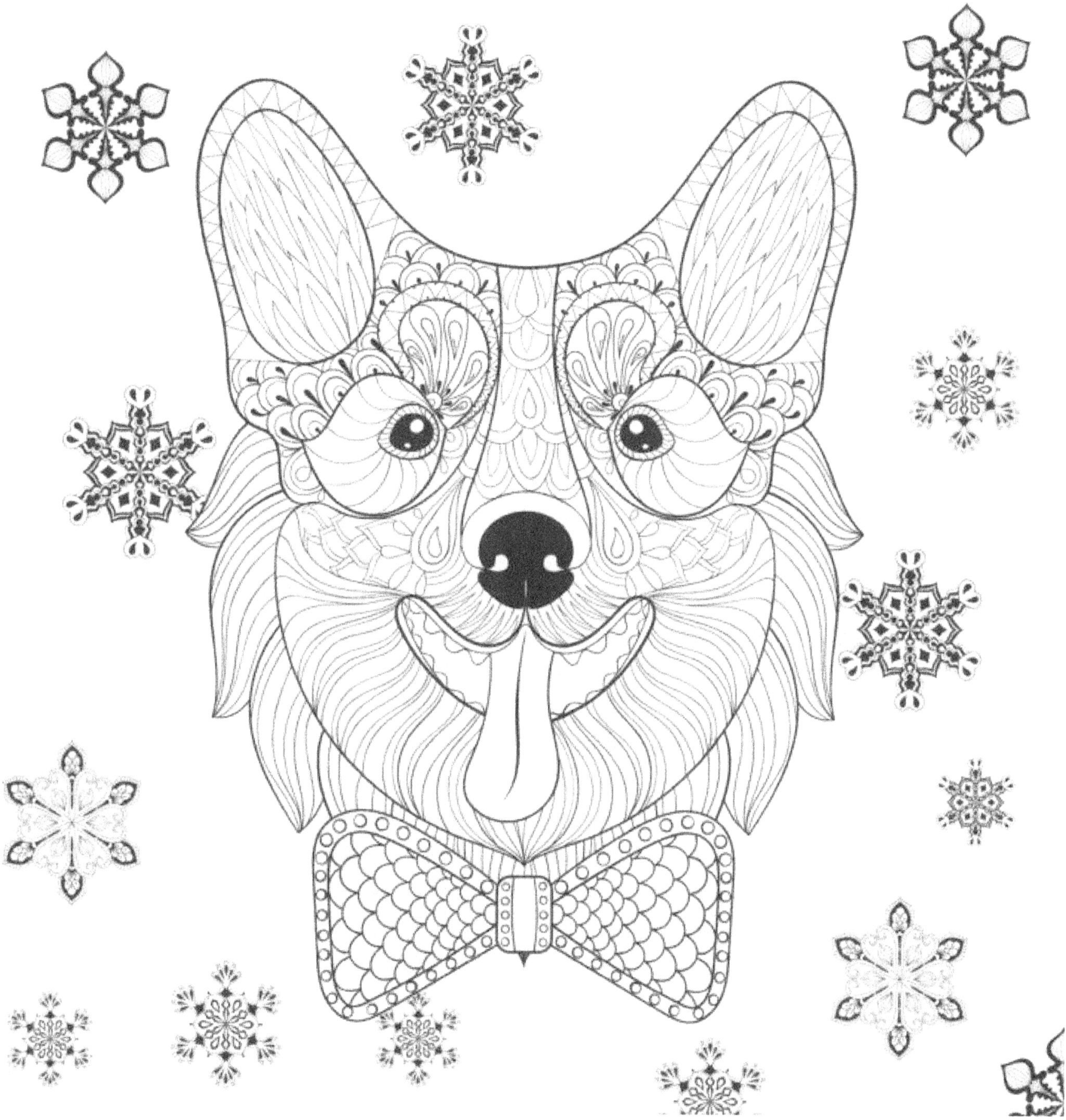

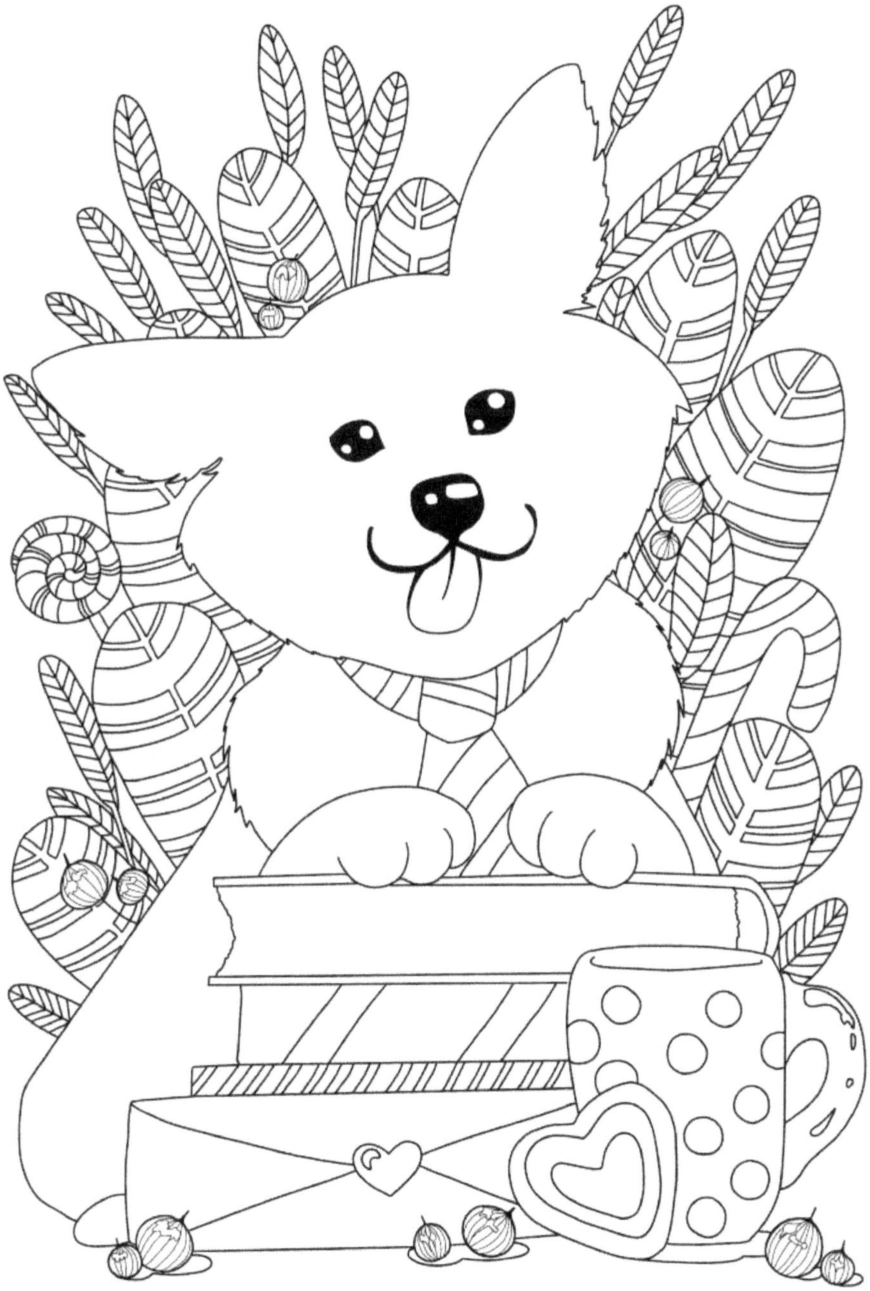

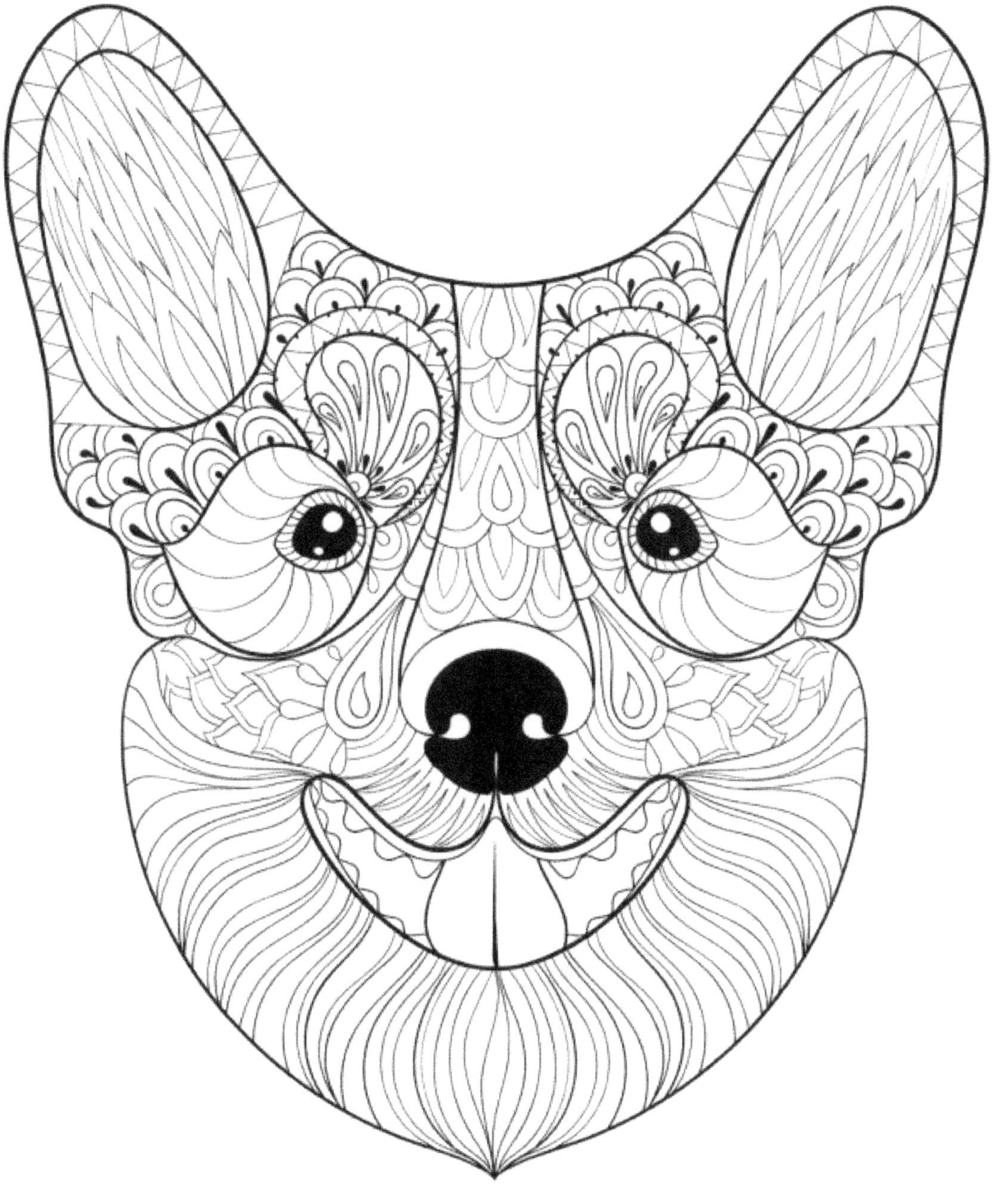

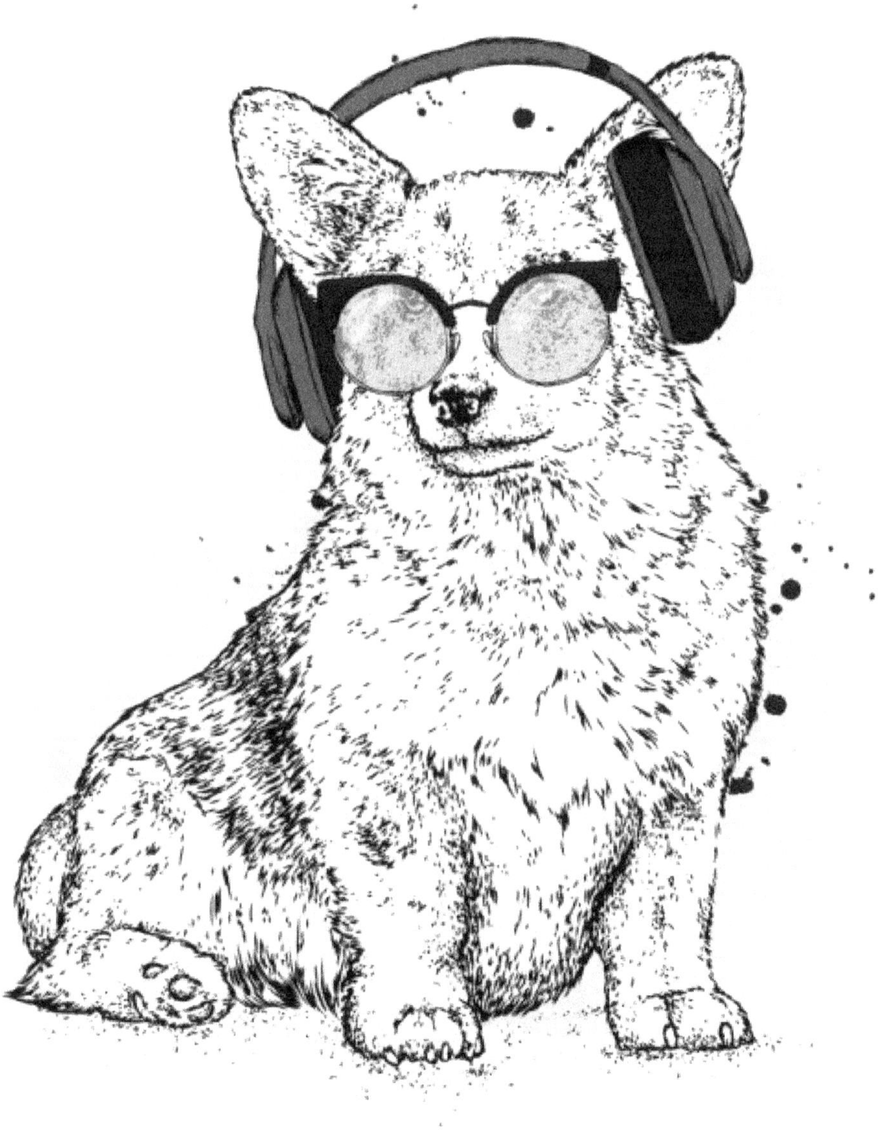

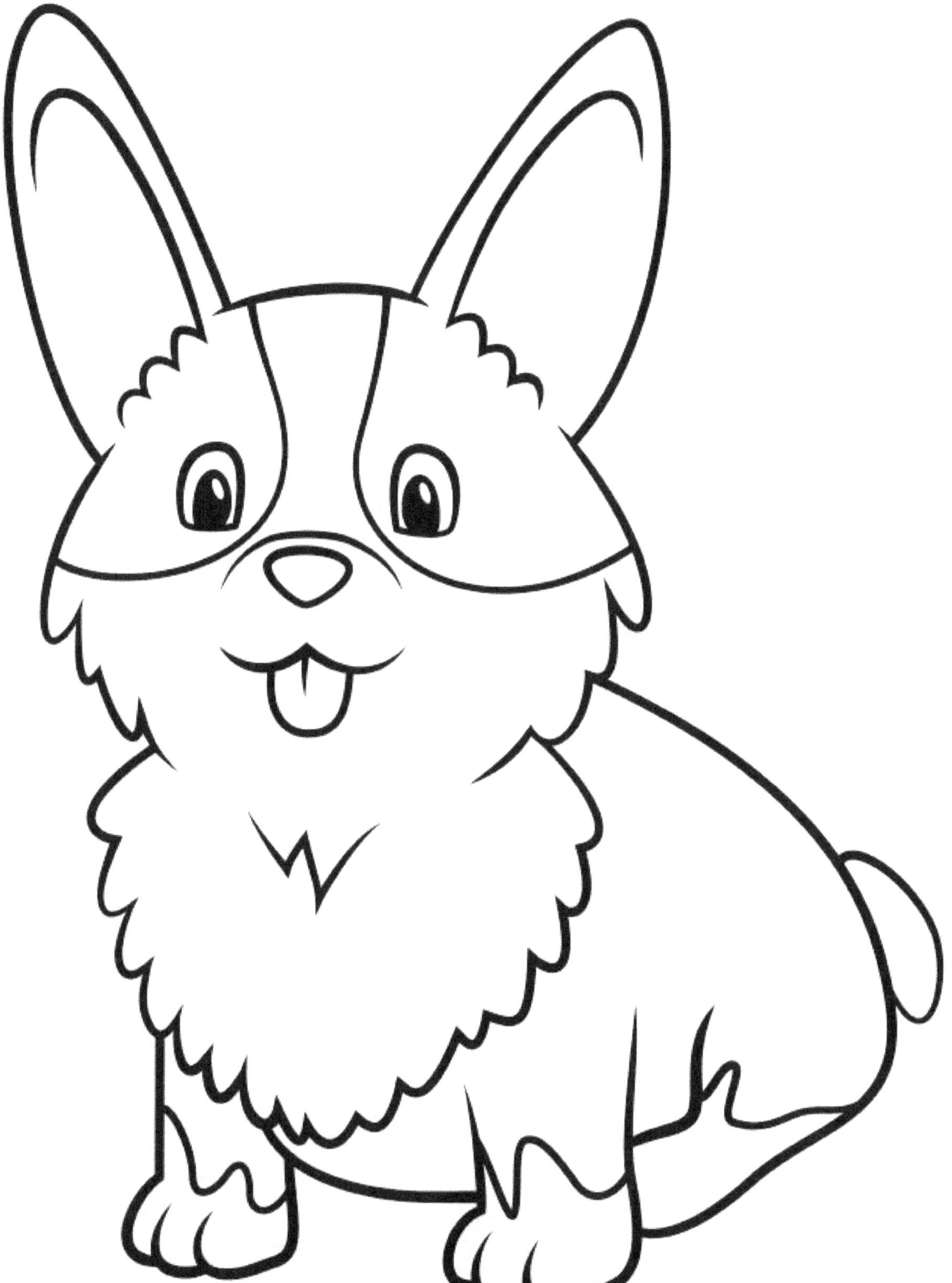

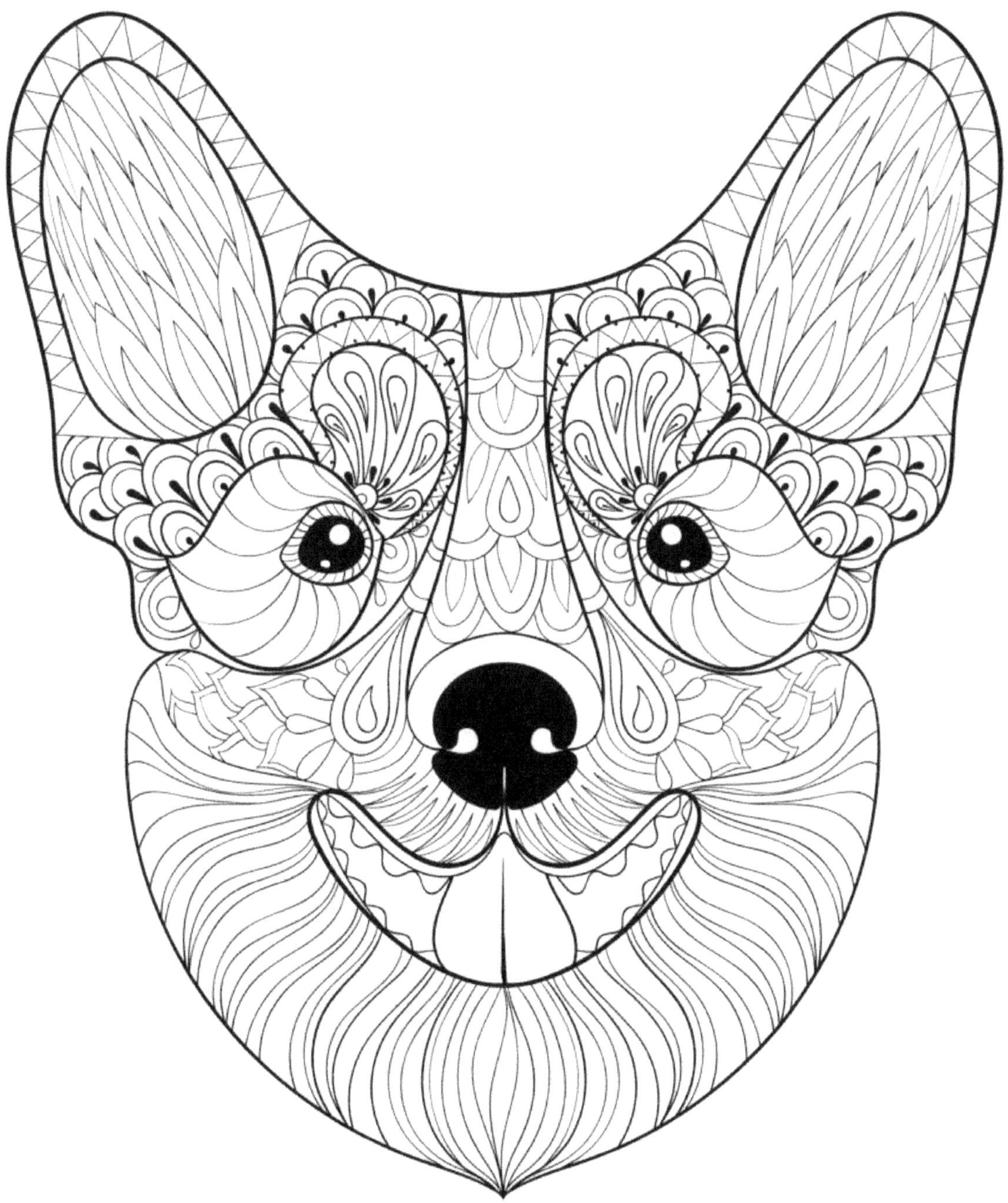

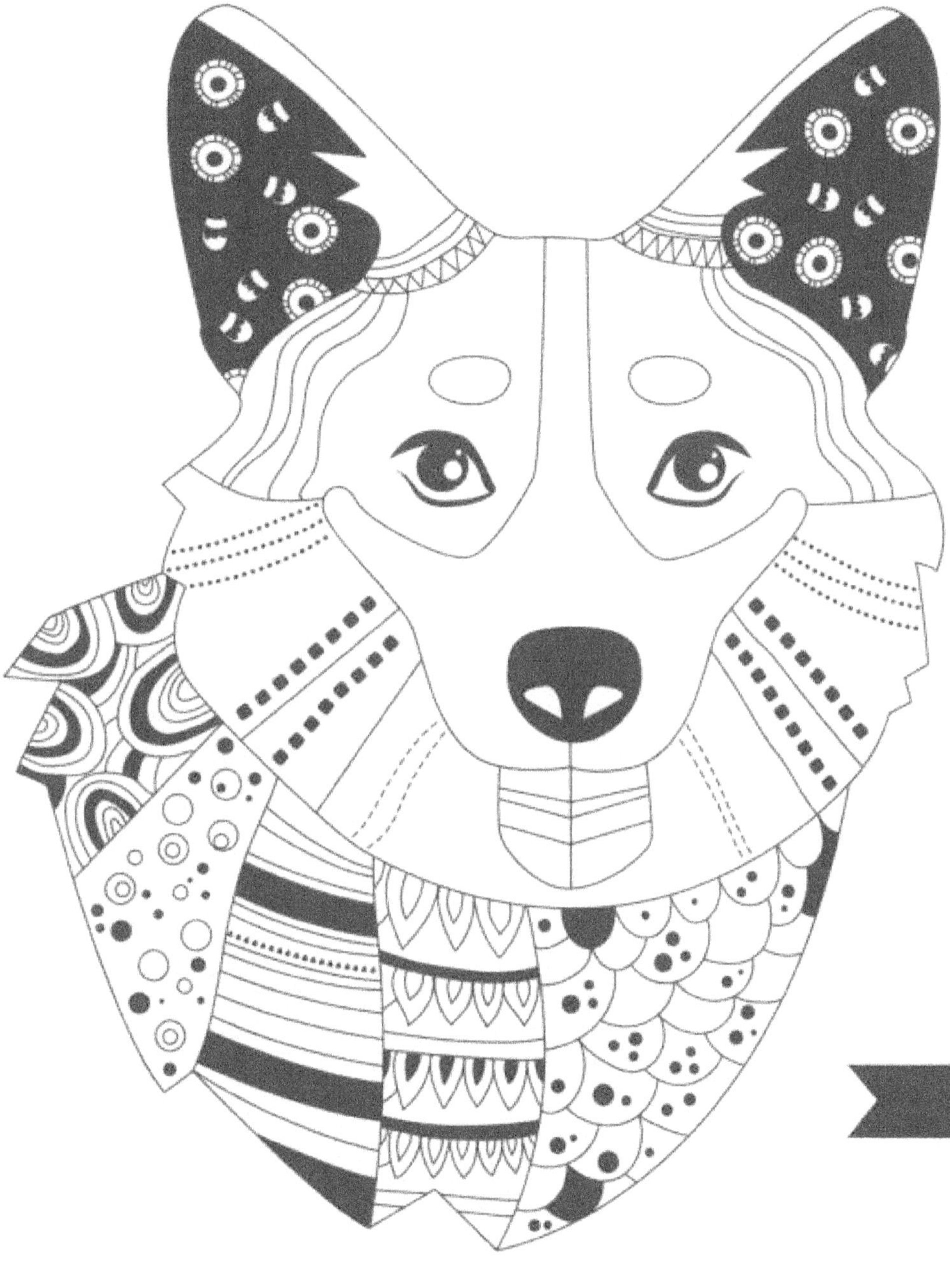

Corgi

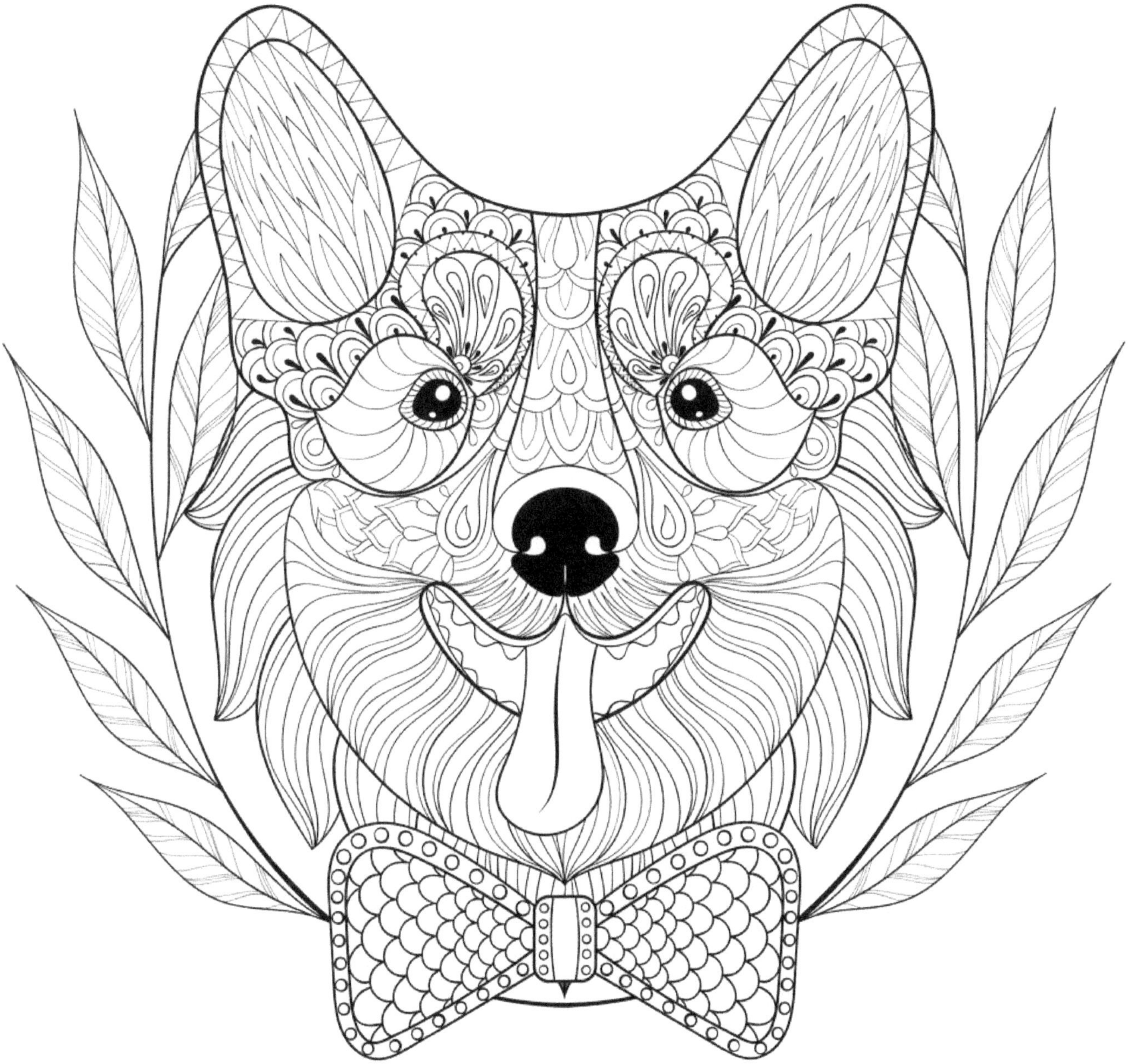

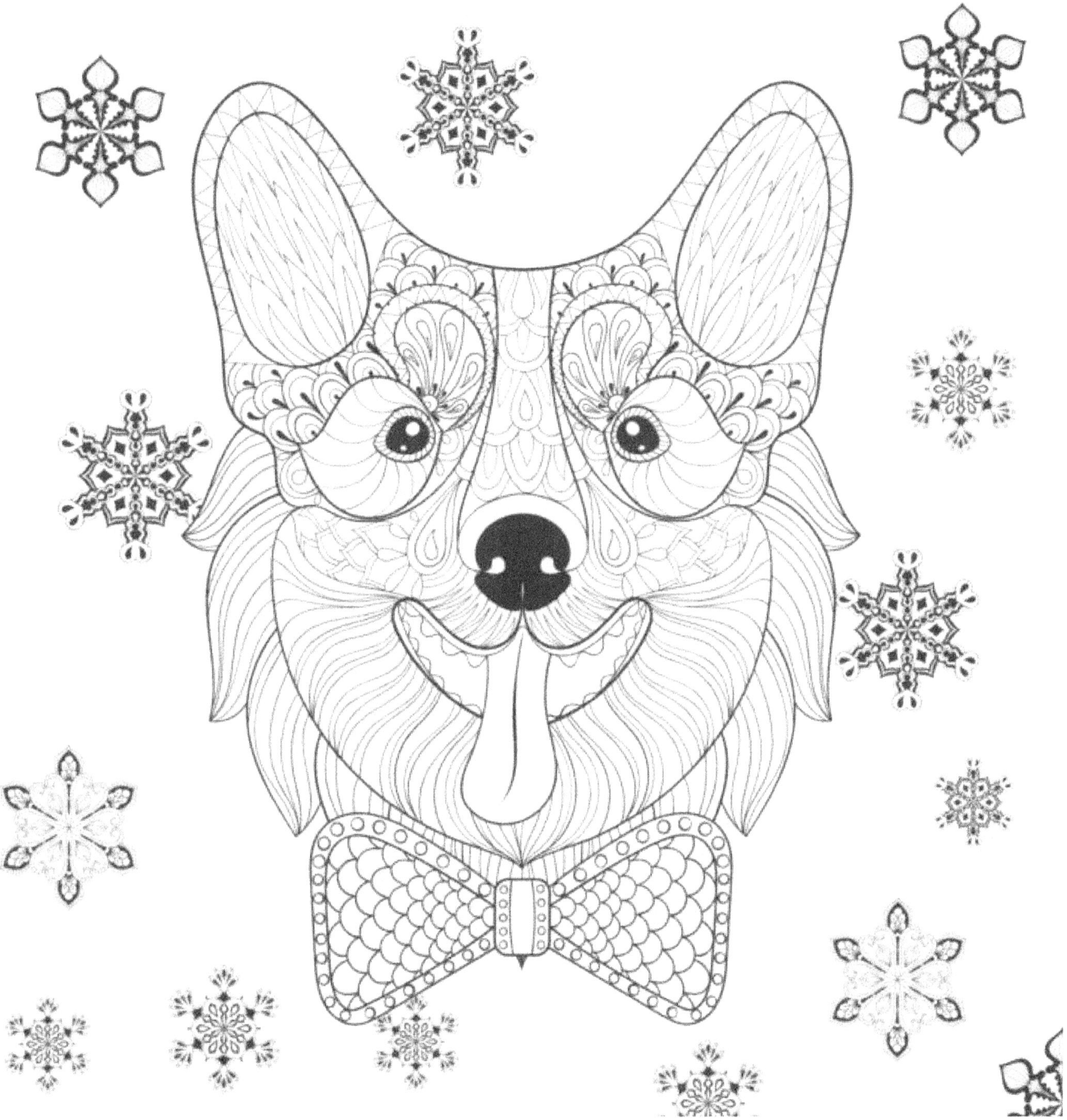

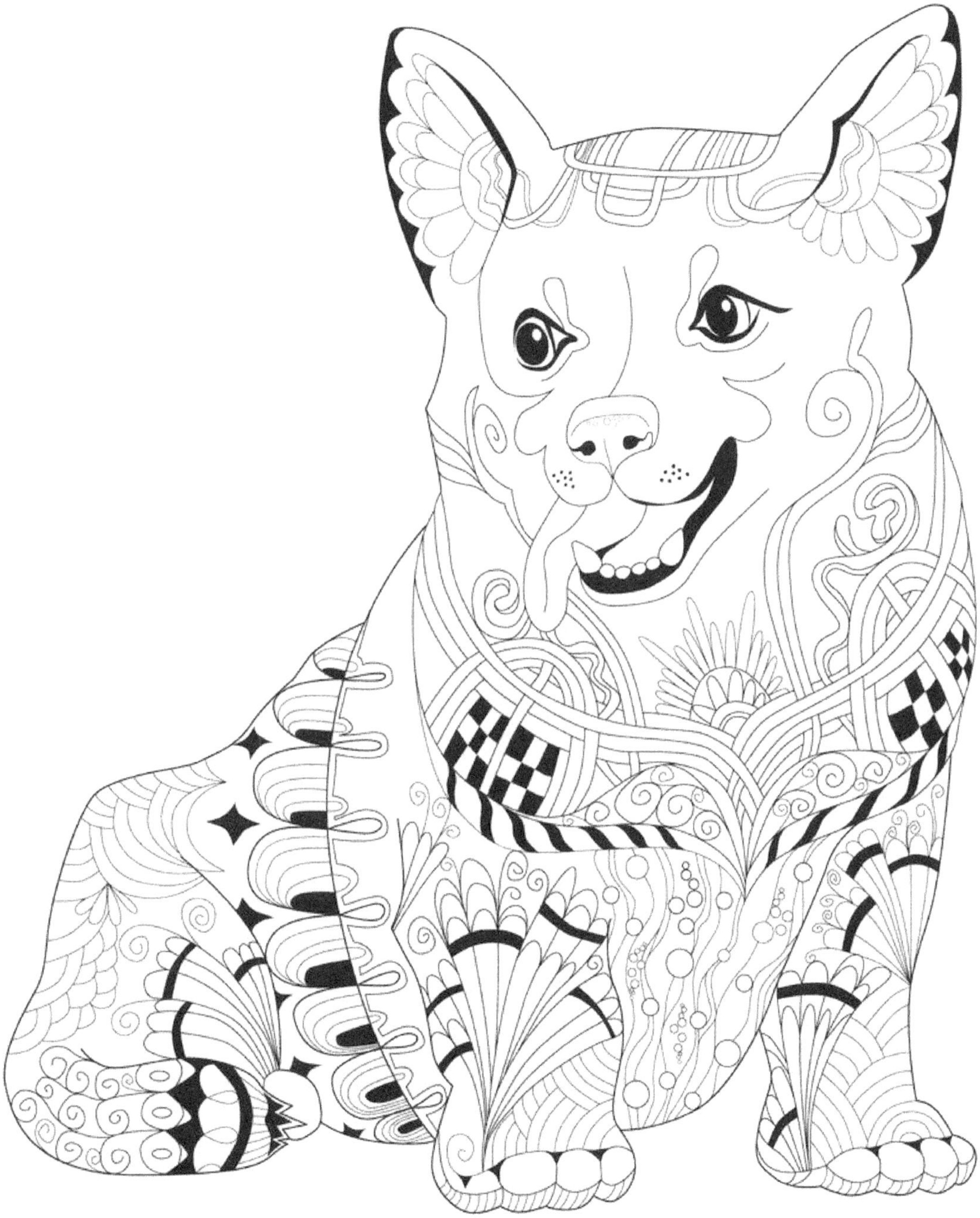

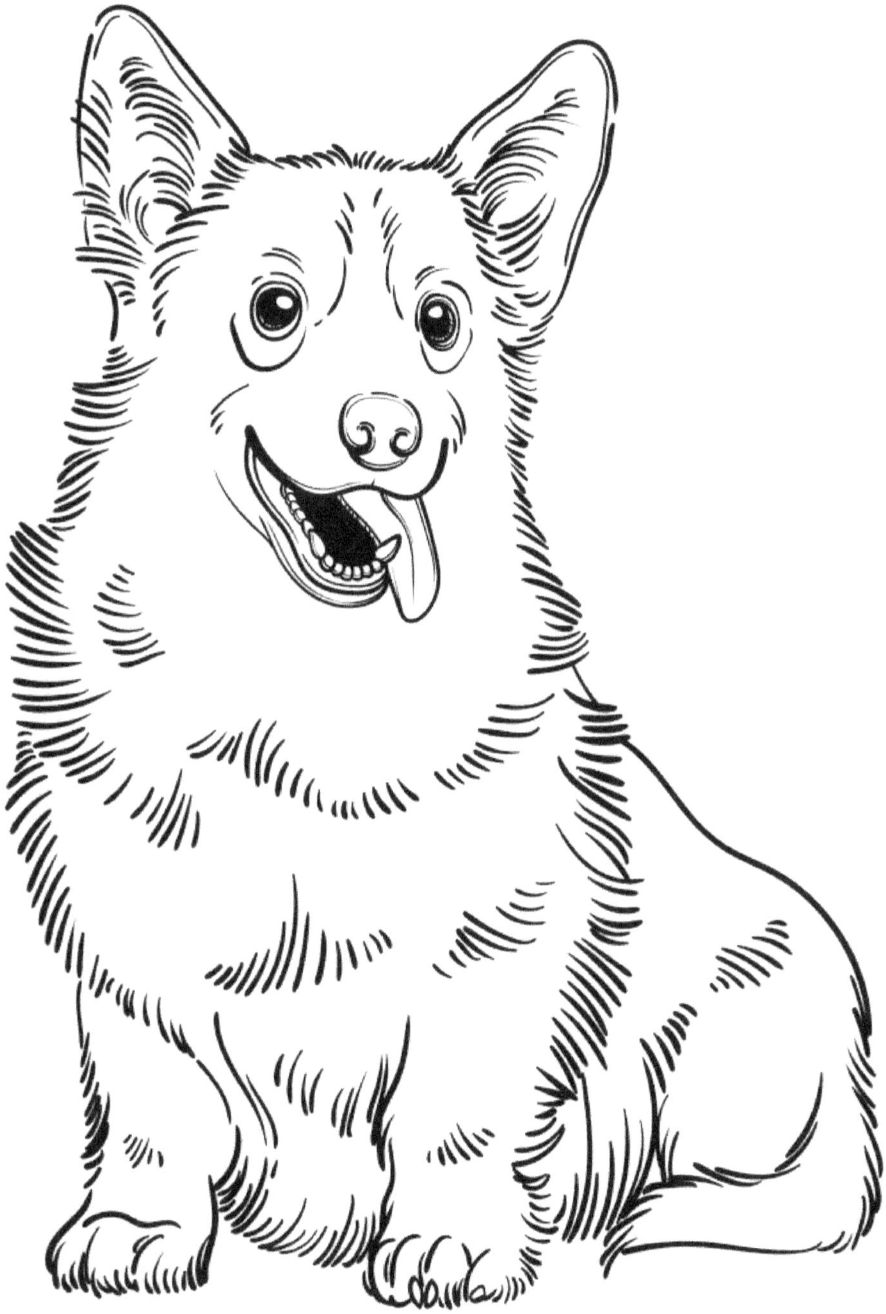

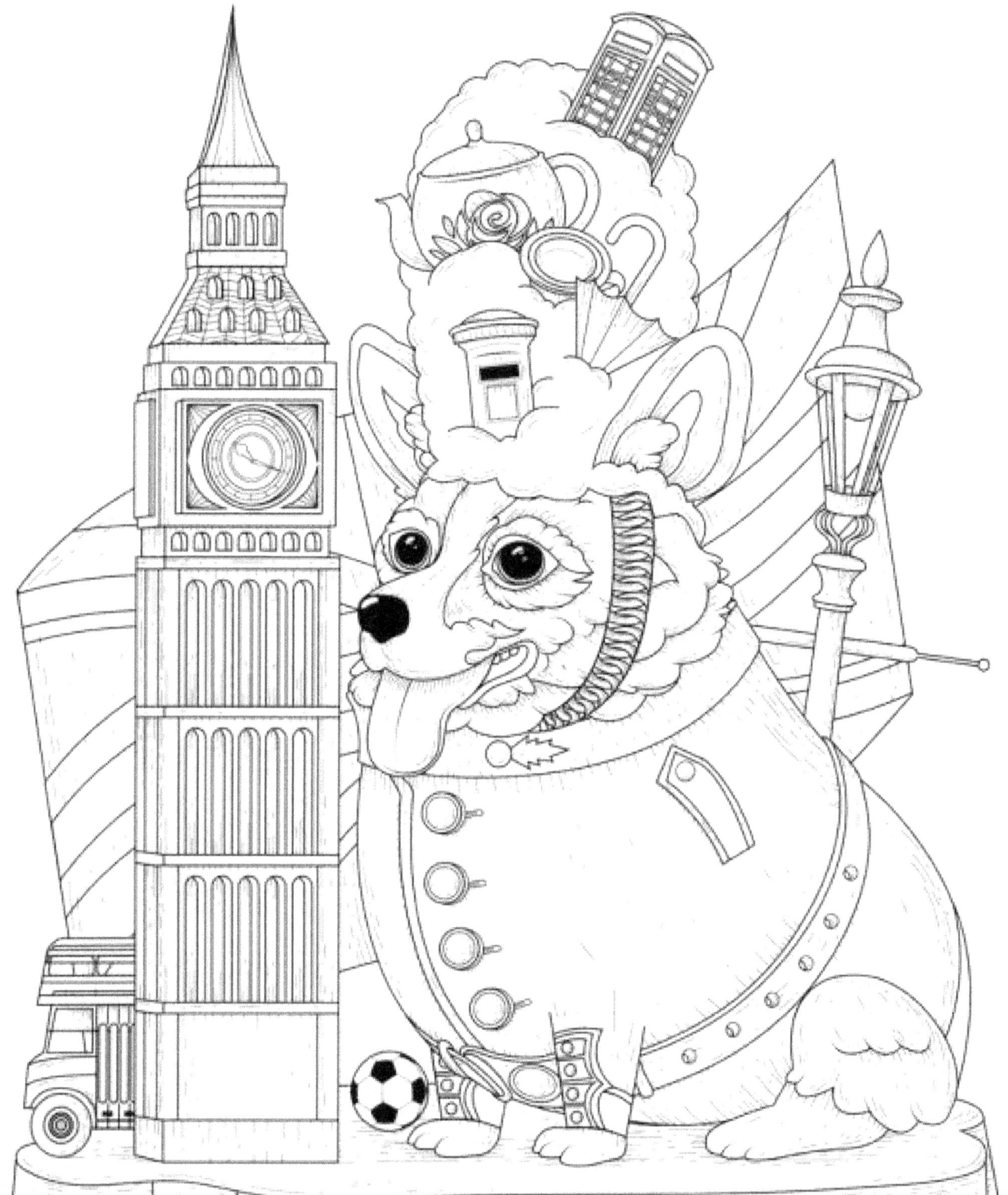

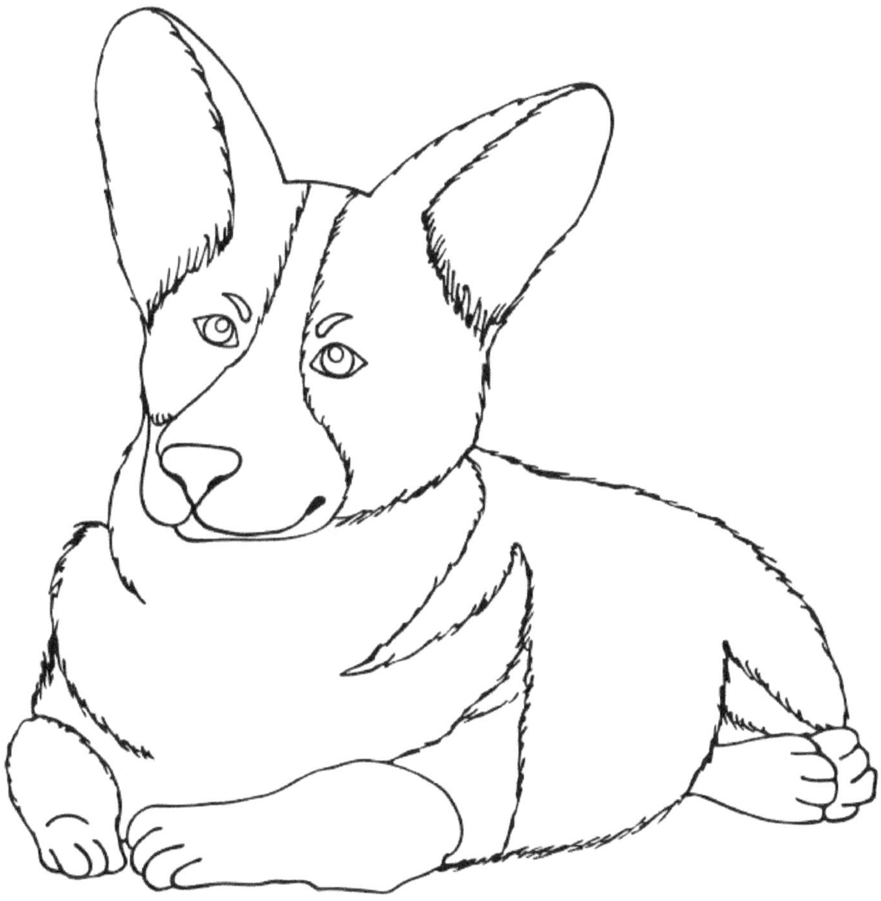

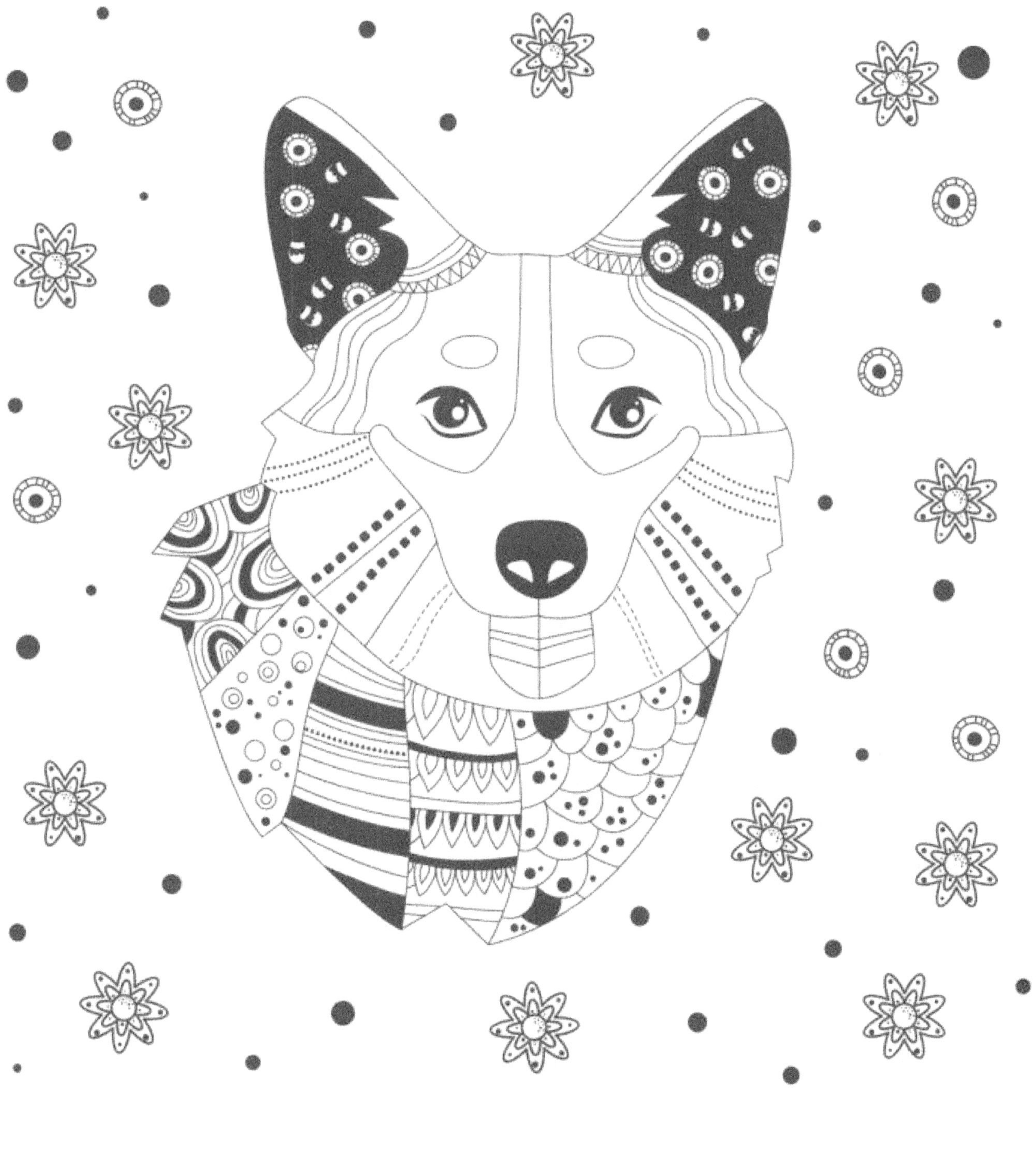

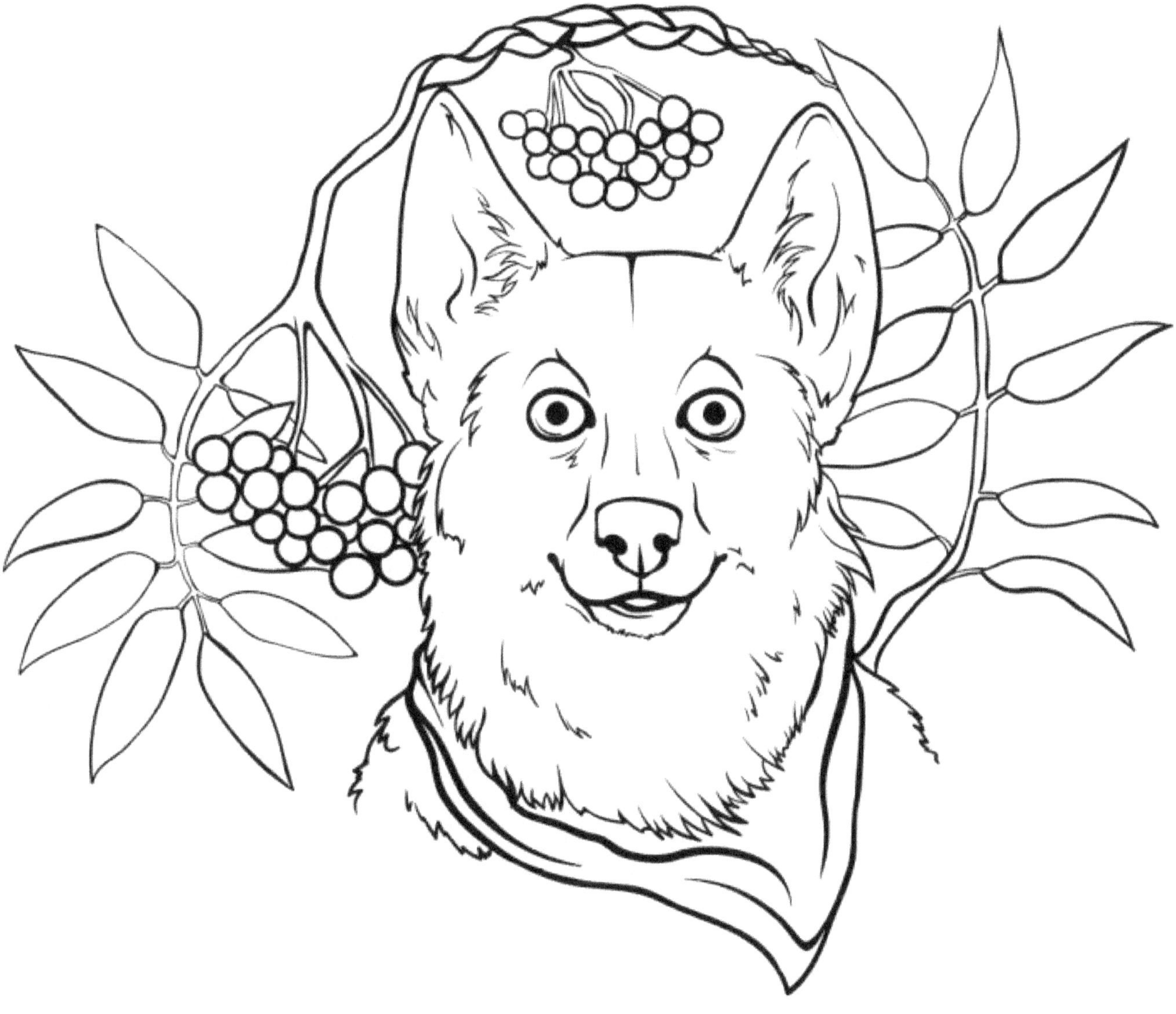

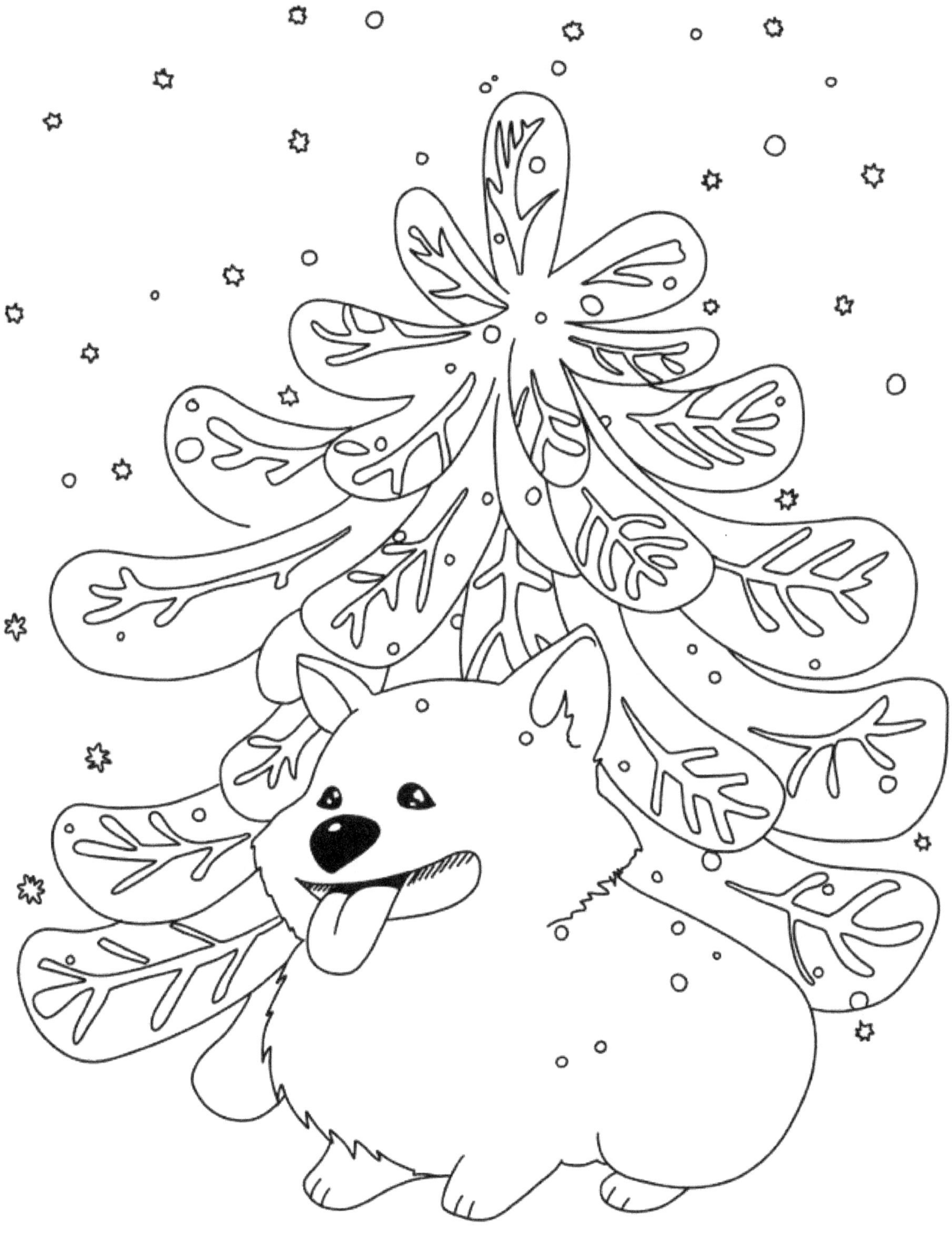

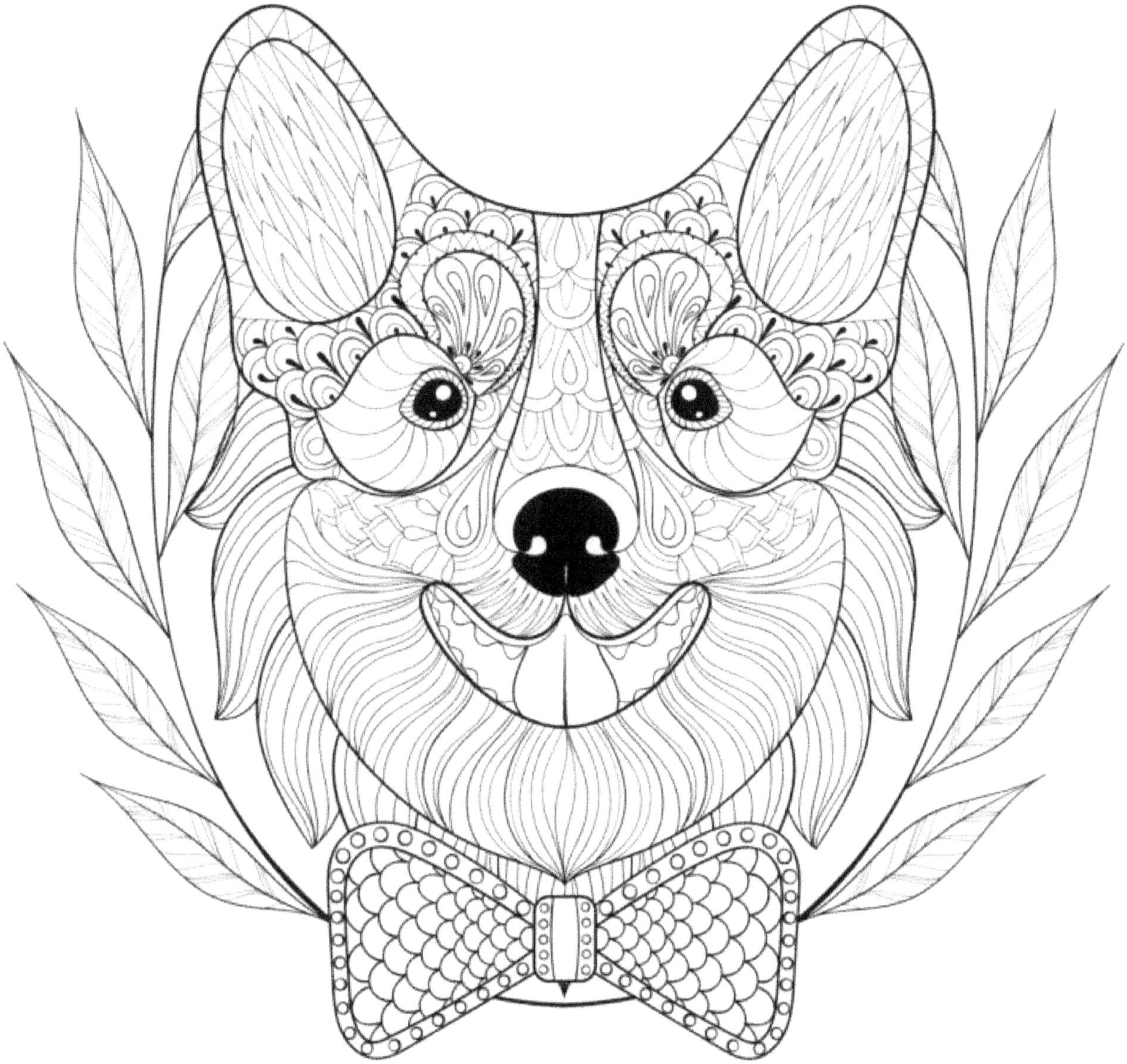

www.ingramcontent.com/pod-product-compliance
Lightning Source LLC
Chambersburg PA
CBHW080627220526
45467CB00011B/3389
* 9 7 9 8 6 8 8 9 9 2 3 4 2 *